Harvest Mice

Text by Beverley Randell

The Smallest Mouse in the World

The harvest mouse is tiny.
It is the smallest mouse in the world.

The harvest mouse has two black eyes
and two small ears.

It has a small nose
and some very long whiskers.

It has four little pink feet
called paws.

And it has a long tail.

Harvest mice are so light that they can climb around in tall grass and wheat.

wheat

They hold on with their tails and their back paws.

What Harvest Mice Eat

Harvest mice eat all kinds of seeds.
They like to eat wheat seeds.

They hold the seeds
in their front paws.

Harvest mice like to eat berries, too.
They eat insects.
They eat new green leaves.

Harvest mice eat **many** things.

Hiding from Danger

Harvest mice are always in danger
because many animals
try to catch them.
Foxes hunt them in the grass.
Owls hunt them from the sky.

But in the summer,
harvest mice have a good place
to hide.

Foxes and owls
cannot see them, or hear them,
in tall, thick wheat.

Building a Nest

Harvest mice build their nests
high up in the wheat,
where they are safe.

The mother mouse
bends some long leaves.
She pulls them around
the wheat stalks
with her teeth and paws.

She works quickly,
and soon the nest
looks like a little ball of grass.

Her babies will be born
inside the nest.

Baby Harvest Mice Grow Fast

A mother harvest mouse has babies
two or three times a year.

The babies are tiny at first,
but they grow every day.
Soon they have coats of fur.

When they are only 15 days old,
they are big enough
to leave the nest!

They can take care of themselves.
They can find all their own food.

Harvest Time

At harvest time, the tiny mice
have to run for their lives.
Big machines come and cut the wheat.

Some of the mice get away,
but some do not.

Getting Through the Winter

After the wheat is cut,
harvest mice try to find new homes.
Sometimes they hide in dry holes,
under bushes, or inside logs.

When the cold winter comes,
it is hard for them to find food,
and many of them die.

But every year, **some** harvest mice
live to see the spring.